It Is a...

LEVEL 1

/c/

DECODABLES BY jump!

Teaching Tips

Pink Level 1

This book focuses on the phoneme **/c/**.

Before Reading

- Discuss the title. Ask readers what they think the book will be about.
- Sound out the words on page 3 together.

Read the Book

- Ask readers to use a finger to follow along with each word as it is read.
- Encourage readers to break down unfamiliar words into units of sound. Then, ask them to string the sounds together to create the words.
- Urge readers to point out when the focused phonics phoneme appears in the text.

After Reading

- Encourage children to reread the book independently or with a friend.
- Ask simple questions about the text to check for understanding. Have them find the pages that have the answers to your questions.

North American adaptations © 2024 Jump!
5357 Penn Avenue South
Minneapolis, MN 55419
www.jumplibrary.com

Library of Congress Cataloging-in-Publication Data is available at www.loc.gov or upon request from the publisher.

ISBN: 979-8-88996-768-2 (hardcover)
ISBN: 979-8-88996-769-9 (paperback)
ISBN: 979-8-88996-770-5 (ebook)

Photo Credits
Images are courtesy of Shutterstock.com. With thanks to Getty Images, Thinkstock Photo and iStockphoto. Cover – TimeImage Production. 4–5 – Lopolo. 6–7 – art nick. 8–9 – xpixel. 10–11 – Happy Author. 14–15 – Shutterstock.

Can you find these words in the book?

cat

not

Is it a cat?

It is not!

Is it a cat?

It is not!

Is it a cat?

It is not!

Is it a cat?

It is a cat!

Can you say this sound and draw it with your finger?

Can you say this word and draw it with your finger?

cat

What other words do you know that start with the letter /c/?

Practice reading the book again:

Is it a cat?

It is not!

Is it a cat?

It is not!

Is it a cat?

It is not!

Is it a cat?

It is a cat!